Divine Message of the Light

Journey of the inner world

KAVITA SHARMA

DEDICATION

To,

Gurudev, Pandit Shri Ram Sharma Acharya Ji
(Founder of "All World Gayatri Parivar")

**"I am not a person,
I am a thought"**

In my Gurudev's words-

"When each one of us takes the responsibility to heal ourselves, we contribute towards healing the world. We create a world full of love, peace, joy, and happiness. Transformation of our thoughts brings transformation in our lives, and we bring heaven onto Mother Earth. Everything depends on our thoughts: the way we think is the way we create our world. Each one of us is responsible for making our world a better place. We, as individuals, can take small steps by bringing positive changes in our thinking- sowing the seeds of positivity and healing our mother Earth."

**"When thoughts change, we change
When we change, the world change"**

"Appo Deepo Bhava"

Thank you, Divine light, my higher
self,
for showing me the pathway
towards life and leading me
to the creation of this book!

CONTENTS

Gratitude

I am deeply grateful for the infinite love of divine universal energies for their blessings and unconditional love.

I am thankful to my parents, brother Gulshan and sister Nisha for their love and encouragement. I am grateful to my husband Amit, for supporting and encouraging me in my healing journey.

Shradha my little angel, thank you for bringing healing and spiritual transformation into my life.

Thank you, my friends, family and teachers for your love and blessings.

Thank you Sounak for helping me with this book.

My heartfelt gratitude to Reena Jain for helping me present this book beautifully to the world and for being a part of my Spiritual journey.

ACKNOWLEDGMENTS

My journey towards this book started with my healing, when I started understanding myself, my life's purpose and why I am here.

When we start healing, we start knowing ourselves, our strengths, our limitations, everything and the first step towards healing is to accept yourself- as you are because nobody is born perfect, similarly, these imperfections taught me where and which aspects of myself needed healing and till then all I needed to do is love those unhealed part of myself because only love can heal us. When there is love, there is healing and when there is healing you discover your true self.

Life is beautiful, but sometimes we get so engrossed in the adversities of our life that we unknowingly start creating suffering and pains for ourselves. We forget that we deserve to be wholesome, and filled with infinite love, joy, and happiness in our life.

Healing came into my life when I needed it the most; I was going through a dark phase of my life. I never thought of healing myself until I became pregnant and felt completely helpless in those 3 months of pregnancy, bedridden with many complications, tried my best but still, I lost my baby.

The miscarriage struck me hard, I was in the cycle of grief, going through depression, sometimes in denial of my reality and other times angry at others and myself, looking for someone to blame (including myself) and crying inconsolably at nights. I withdrew myself completely from social life; still trying to figure out what just happened to me. This incident shook me to the core and made my suffering even more intense.

Each day was difficult for me, I was unable to find any reason to wake up in the morning, spending my time watching web series and waiting to sleep again. I had no idea how can I come out of my grief because now my pain was unbearable and made me look at life hopelessly with no reason to live. I felt as if I lost some part of myself, felt miserable thinking that I was unable to save my baby and emptiness was all I could feel.

After every night, there comes dawn and soon I too saw some light when I tried to find out the reason for my miscarriage through a Hypnotherapy session.

My purpose for this session was completely different from what I experienced in that life-changing moment when I encountered my Gurudev standing as my Spirit Guide, who pour his healing light and was filling my heart with divine, unconditional love and that was the moment I felt that I am not alone, My Gurudev, the entire universe is there with me, looking after me, loving me, guiding me to a new journey of spirituality.

At that moment I realized that all along I was living a meaningless life and then spirituality entered my life, it brought a deep and meaningful purpose to my life.

My Gurudev helped me see the light at the end of the tunnel and I started walking towards that light knowing that my Spirit Guide is there with me, supporting me, and showing me the path towards my healing journey. When we feel divine forces standing with us, protecting, and guiding us; then a sense of hope and faith develops within us and the same happened with me. I started my spiritual journey with complete trust, faith, and belief and my Gurudev too showered his blessings and presented me with the most precious gift for my spiritual journey- ***Gayatri***

Mantra.

And now when looking back, since then at every step which I have taken including writing this book, the Gayatri mantra was my strength. It has not only pulled me out of the darkness I was in but also opened a lot of doors towards my spiritual journey.

Within a year I was blessed with a lovely daughter, and everything happened under the guidance of Gurudev's astral presence and with the most precious spiritual gift: **Gayatri Mantra**. This powerful Vedmantra helped me release my pain, healed me, and blessed me with a child. I will always be grateful for the divine presence of **Gayatri Mata** (Mother Divine) in my life.

I thought with the birth of my daughter, my movie was over, but then I realized that the real spiritual journey has now begun for me. My motive behind practicing Gayatri Mantra was not just for fulfilling my materialistic need, I found peace while reciting the mantra and it made me move ahead in my spiritual journey.

Gayatri Mantra helped me in the purification of my mind, body, and soul. The divine presence of Gayatri Mata gave me everything and more than anything I felt a deep, unconditional love, a love which can heal anything and everything. I could find my peace within, which I was looking outside.

My spiritual journey is still going on and will keep on progressing ahead till I am alive. I hope this book reaches everyone who is seeking healing, divine light, infinite love, and peace.

May you all be free from all the pain and suffering you

might be going through and heal and find the source of infinite love which is within you.

"When the darkness prevails outside,
I am the ray of hope inside.

When you search for me in temples and church,
I am present in every creation of the universe.

When you fight for me in the name of religion, I try to
teach humanity over every religion.

When you display hatred and greed, I spread messages
of love and compassion.

When you blame me for all the destruction,
I will show you the mirror of introspection.

When you want to change the world, I teach you to
change yourself first.

When you start bringing change within yourself, I will
create a paradise for you in this world."

I

LOVE THYSELF

Self-love is about loving thyself; loving others; accepting yourself; giving yourself a little more love, a little more patience, and a little more care. We all are infinite beings, filled with love. We need to recognize that love and fill our hearts with that love. We all deserve love. Love is a pure energy, a pure vibration.

We all come with a bucket of love and slowly start filling this love bucket with criticism, disappointments, and others' limiting beliefs and opinions. We must remember that our identity is not based merely on each other's opinion or the judgement we pass on each other.

We all are infinite beings. We are everything that the universe is or possesses. We need to look within ourselves, we all need to discover ourselves and that is our journey: **a journey of self-love.**

Where does this love disappear when we grow up?

It keeps fading because of others' judgement. You give others more importance. Isn't it? You think they know you better than yourself. You give the key of self-love to another hand. This is all your responsibility. You need to take back that key.

You need to take back that power which you give others to control you. You are your own master of love, abundance and prosperity. Don't give that power to others to judge and control who you are. You know yourself better than anyone else can. You need to realize your worth.

Always remember that you are an infinite being coming to this planet in the form of a body, but you are more than your body. You are a soul; a beautiful soul, a powerful soul, a pure soul. You are love and only love.

How to find this love?

Fill your heart with love, pure love, coming from the universe. Feel the love pouring into your heart. Feel a divine white light spreading in your heart, filling you with compassion, kindness, bliss, peace, happiness, and abundance.

Now feel that love in every breath that you take. Let that love radiate to the world. Let it flow through you to others and the world. Radiate your love to the world. Let everyone soak in this love. Let this world, our earth, be a loving place. Each one of us needs to contribute to healing our earth and it starts with loving ourselves. Everything starts with love. Love dissolves everything: war, hatred, jealousy, anger, ...

Whenever you feel alone, imagine a divine white light pouring into your heart, filling your heart with immense love. You don't have to seek love from others. You are loved. Let those loving energy fill the world with love and let its presence make you a loving being. Divine love is always there. You just need to feel it, smell it, hear it, and sense it!

Just remember to be kind to yourself first and then shower that kindness on others. You are a loving being. You radiate love. You glow in love. You soak in love.
"Love is the beauty which fills everything with abundance."

2
FINDING LOVE

We are love beings. Love sometimes fades from our life due to certain external circumstances. But instead of finding it outside, find it within. You are full of love. Shed those negative beliefs blocking you to love yourself and others. How can you shed it?

Appreciate yourself every day: Look at the mirror and affirm: **"I love you"** to yourself thrice. Look deep within your eyes, and feel that love for yourself.

"I am love.
I love myself.
I love myself completely.
I love myself as I am.
I accept myself as I am.
I am love."

Feel that love in your eyes for yourself. Do it every day. It won't take much time. Your subconscious mind will listen to it and it will change its programming to *"Love Thyself"*.

Believe in yourself: Trust yourself, have faith in yourself, in your ability and in your potential. As we grow up, we start losing our confidence and belief by listening to others and their opinion about us. We listen to others' judgment and hence start losing our self-belief because of criticism by others.

These words keep haunting us throughout our life, diminishing our confidence more and more and hence we try to live a simple life where we don't want to do anything challenging. We become habituated to living in our comfort zone so that we don't want to try something new.

Hence, we start avoiding such situations where we are challenged and face obstacles. But we never think that these challenges can lead us to beautiful destinations, bringing a new ray of hope in our life just by a leap of faith, in ourselves and Divinity.

We should not forget that we are born equals with equal capabilities; some discover it sooner and some later. Some face their life challenges themselves, facing everything head-on and others are in flight mode (running from our situations). We give up easily. But have you ever thought, what can go wrong?

Would you lose your life if you don't succeed, or your life will become dull? It is anyway dull and meaningless. Now think about your challenges. Are you willing to come out of your comfort zone? The result can be either you will be proud of yourself, or, if you fail, you will know that at least you tried and gave your effort, and it taught you a life lesson.

We need to face our fear upright and overcome that fear with faith and self-belief.
Love yourself enough, believe in yourself enough.

Give yourself the credit; acknowledge it as you deserve it. Allow your soul to bloom with faith.

Declare:
I believe in myself.
I believe in the supreme creation of God and hence I believe in myself.
I am capable.
I trust myself.
I trust my abilities to succeed in life.

Know your importance: Be like an eagle, who knows how to fly alone, trusting in its ability. Eagle always teaches us to focus on our goals and believe in our abilities. They are ambitious to fly high in the sky without restricting themselves and are always open to receiving messages from the vast universe.

Be like an eagle
Know your importance
Be Limitless
Be proactive
Be brave
Be strong
Be goal-oriented
Be strong
Be powerful
Be like an eagle
And fly high.

Take your power back: We are all born as limitless and powerful beings but with time we give away our power to situations and people if they know us better than ourselves. Especially if we face any challenge in our life, we quickly absorb the messages of others (their opinion) and a limitless person is lost at that very moment.

Imagine how many times you have listened to others and given away your power or just because you failed once in life, you gave up in life, considering yourself a failure. It's time to take back your power. Recognize your worth and be who you were born to be.

I am sure that if you are born, there must be some reason. Isn't it? We are born not just to eat, sleep and repeat. There must be some higher purpose. There must be some reason that you are incarnated on Earth. There must be a lesson you have come to learn. What is that lesson?

That is upon you to explore as we all have different lessons to learn based on our growth. But we must remember that each one has something important to do. We are not simply born to count our days and finish up our daily chores. These are part of our life but not our entire life purpose.

Think about your life purpose. Think about being a powerful being, born here to do something extraordinary in our unique way (not based on others' beliefs). Be who you are by realizing your power.

Listen to yourself, your inner child: Let your inner

child come out. Play with your inner child. It knows how to make you feel loved again. It knows what you need. Absorb that innocence of your inner child. It will help you to love yourself back again. Hold on to your inner child. Acknowledge your inner child's worth. Give your inner child the love that it needs.

Connecting with your inner child
Bring both your hands to your heart space. Visualize a five-year-old version of yourself. Now call your inner child to connect with you. Visualize your inner child filling your heart with love, happiness, and joy.

Let that feeling of joy pass through your entire body, starting from your heart to your entire body. And you will start radiating with love, pure, unconditional love. Talk to your inner child; give your time and presence to him/her.

Ask him what he wants. What does it need? Fulfil its little demand, those demands are not unnecessary, it knows what you want will make you feel loved. It only demands love. You can at least give it love. Can't you? It's that simple. But you must take out that time; you need to invest in yourself every day.

Let your inner child play with you and always say thank you to your inner child.

Thank you, my inner child,
With all your love.

I love you.
Your inner child is the most beautiful and
radiant being full of love.
You will love connecting with it

3

HEALING

Healing is a deep process; a process to heal not only our body but also our mind and soul. We all are a part of divine power (Universe) and to heal one is to return to that divine power which resides in each and every one of us. So, to heal is to be yourself again, to remove all the past conditioning, our limited beliefs, and thoughts, all the pain and sorrow that is stored within us needs to be released.

To heal is to dig deep into oneself.
Healing is not limited to only this lifetime; it is beyond time and space, beyond everything. Healing is all about embracing once again who we are.

Who are you?
Do we know who we are in reality?
Are you your mind?
Are you your body?
Are you your name?
No
You are beyond all that. You are yourself. You are your originality. You are pure. You are love. You are divine as you are from a divine being. You are free. You are powerful. You are beautiful in every aspect regardless of your age, gender, caste, etc. You are beautiful as you are.

To heal yourself is to heal your true essence. You

need to understand your own magic. Firstly, start accepting yourself as you are: remember that you are love, you are pure. Accept who you are. Accept yourself in order to heal. You need to first accept yourself, and then you need to work on your body, then on emotions and shedding old conditionings.

Layers of emotions
We are surrounded by many layers, which are not our facts. They have come from our old habits, addictions and from what others have told us since our childhood, and we have imbibed all these within us.

Consider yourself as a lotus flower, with closed petals and as those petals are opened it blooms into a beautiful flower. Similarly, we too need to open all those layers, to know our true self, our originality and how beautiful we are.

Healing is not a one-day process. It takes time. It's messy, it's fun, it's loving, it's sad at times as we have to embrace everything about ourselves, we can't run. If you are ready, then this journey begins here:

❖ **Accept yourself**, your limitations, your flaws, your nature, your strengths, your weaknesses, accept it. Accept yourself totally.
I accept myself completely
I am whole now.
I am a whole loving being

❖ Start **being grateful** for little things in life. Those little things will unlock great things for you.

Once you start being grateful to your life, your family, your work, to yourself, your body; miracles will start happening. You will start attracting abundance. But in order to do so, stop your complaining habit. I know it's hard, but you need to stop complaining, it will not lead you anywhere. It's a waste of time. So, stop complaining and start being grateful.

What can you be grateful for?
Your health. Aren't you neglecting your health? Aren't you taking your body for granted? Take some time out to be thankful to your body. Your body will love you for that. Your body is your temple, reside beautifully in it. Don't abuse it or take it for granted.

❖ **Give time to yourself**: Involve yourself in constructive things, which you love doing. Ask yourself what do you want to do? Whether you want to read, write, sing, dance, or anything else that you always wanted to do and just do it.

We often neglect our interest and keep avoiding it. But if you are not happy yourself then how can you make others happy? This is a very small step, but very important for the sake of your happiness. Dig out one little thing from your inside that you want to do for yourself, it can be anything and just do it.

❖ **Meditate:** It's very important to keep our mind and body peaceful and it can only be done through meditation. It is a vitamin for the soul. Just like food and water is very important for your body, similarly meditation is very important for your soul. Once you start meditating you will start seeing results on your own.

Start with five minutes a day. It can be any guided meditation or meditating on any God or divine power you believe in. You will experience peace and happiness like never before. It will help you in connecting with your own self. Try it for once, for yourself, for your own happiness.

Make meditation an important part of your life. You will never feel alone again. A deep bond will start forming with divine God, our source of infinite love.

❖ **Grounding:** Always remember to stay grounded. Grounding is very important because it will help you remain centered; you will not be worried unnecessarily. It will also help you to remain in the present moment. Simple grounding exercises can be done such as gardening, dancing, cleaning, sitting on ground, walking barefoot, etc. So ground your energy by walking amid nature.

❖ **Breath:** *Breath in and breath out*

We are so busy in our day-to-day life, that we forget to deep breathing. Deep breathing is important not only for physical health, but also for our mental health as well.

Breath in positivity and happiness and breathe out all your worries and stress.

Breathing consciously is important to stay connected with our present. We are often thinking about our past or worrying about our future. But is it going to change our past or future?

No, you can't change your past and your future is uncertain. So be present and enjoy where you are. And to stay present, we can simply breath in and breath out. Start with doing it 10 times.

Sit and relax and take a deep breath in and breath out.
Breath in all the positivity, all the love from the infinite source of love (God).
Breath out all the worry and sadness.

Try at least 10 times. If you know *Pranayama (breathing exercise)* then do that, it will be very beneficial. But for now, start with *deep breathing* and see the magic.

Life is beautiful. We often forget to realize that so many beautiful things are present in this world. Take a moment to enjoy it and express your gratitude towards it. We are all full of love, happiness, joy, prosperity, abundance, and peace. Everything resides here, with time we have lost it somewhere. Try finding it once again. Try to find it inside you, not outside of you and you will soon find it but with patience and kindness towards yourself.

Always remember that healing takes time. So treat yourself with a little extra love every day and with a little extra care. Even if you snap to your old mode, be patient and loving to yourself.

It's ok! You are doing great
Pause and appreciate yourself for all your efforts
You are doing great
You are a wonderful creation of God, and its creation (you) is as beautiful as God.
I am kind towards myself and others
I am loving towards myself and others
I appreciate myself everyday
I am proud of myself

4
DUALITIES OF MIND AND BODY

Our body is the storehouse of all our emotions, feelings, thoughts, and actions. It stores literally everything you say or feel in any situation whether we realize it or not.

Every time we say something negative about ourselves, it gets stored within our body. How does it get stored? In the form of an illness (either temporary or permanent). Whatever we say and think about ourselves, has a profound effect on our body.

Our body is our shield to safeguard us from heavy emotions and sometimes while protecting us, it results in a rise of an illness. It is not our body's fault. How long can it protect us from our own negative feelings, if again and again we keep saying to it, "you are worthless", "you are an idiot", etc.

These statements get stored deep inside us, leaving a permanent scar within us leading to form an illness, which can be either temporary or permanent, depending upon the intensity of those emotions and for long we have been saying such negative statements to us.

Mind and body Connection

Our body is our temple where the soul resides. Our soul is the only thing which we possess and hence we must keep good care of our body. It needs our attention in order to stay healthy and fit. Every Time, it tries to signal whenever we go wrong i.e. we start thinking negative or self-destructive thought, or negative feelings. We need to be aware of our body.

Body awareness

We are so busy with our thought that it starts drowning us into negativity and we are not even aware of it. We keep drowning and drowning into the sea of sorrow, misery, fears, doubts, anxiety, sadness and so on. Sometimes even after being aware that we are drowning, we cannot help ourselves because we are already at a point where we cannot save ourselves.

This is what our mind does every time it is free to do its work, free to lead us into negativity. Here we need to stop this cycle if we want to save ourselves from drowning (into misery and negativity).

Hence at regular interval we need to be aware and alert of our body, of our breathing, of our heartbeats which are teaching us to be present and thus we can give some attention to our body and stop that cycle of negativity to affect our mind and body, leading to physical and mental illnesses. So, it is our foremost responsibility towards us to be aware of what is happening inside. The moment we are aware, the mind loses its power, and we take back our power by bringing our attention.

By being aware of what is happening inside (our body), we can heal what is happening outside. So, in order to heal outside, we must focus inside. And the story of our life starts changing for good.
We are here to live a peaceful, happy, and healthy life, not a life full of misery.

Hence, we need to take steps; we need to take control in our hand instead of going on autopilot mode. **Be aware**: every time, every moment of your breath.

At regular intervals, try to focus on your breath, on your heartbeat, listen to the beautiful rhythm of your heartbeat; you will love it once you start listening.

When you start focusing inside your body with the power of your presence, you will start loving your body, thereby dissolving all the ailments slowly and slowly.

Body awareness exercise

Take a deep breath in and breathe out. Feel a wave of freshness and positivity entering inside you and as you breathe out, observe all your worries, anxiety, fear, negativity going out. Once again

take a deep breath in and breath out. (Repeat 5 times)
Now slowly feel your body relaxing from your feet going towards your entire leg. Feel a wave of relaxation going upward from your legs to your knees, your thigh towards your lower abdomen, your belly, slowly flowing towards your chest, listen to your heartbeat, feel the love from your heart flowing to each cell of your body.

Feel a wave of happiness flowing in your body. Feel your neck getting relaxed, going towards your face, and slowly passing towards your head and thereby going at the back of your body. Your shoulders and arms are getting relaxed; your back is getting relaxed. Now again take a deep breath in and breath out.

This is a simple relaxation exercise to help you to be present; to be in the here and now. Whenever you lose focus, start focusing on your inside. Feel this presence, feel this stillness which is present inside of

5
ANGER & FEAR

Anger is an uninvited visitor that suddenly comes knocking at our door and it is always unpleasant to welcome this visitor. Suddenly all the accumulated feelings come up like a tide of waves ready to drown you in it or anyone present near you. So, it becomes important to acknowledge our anger whenever it comes and peel away the layers of emotions hidden behind anger.

You will be surprised what you may find out as there are so many emotions suppressed within you which never got an outlet assuming it be invalidated or will not be approved by others if you show your emotions. Hence you have kept accumulating piles of emotions and feelings.

There is baggage, heavy baggage that you carry and once you start opening it, you might find criticism, guilt, shame, grief, fear (fear of abandonment, fear of persecution, fear of separation, etc.), disappointment and many more.

We all have tried to suppress our anger every time it comes up as we consider it socially unacceptable but if we embrace the baggage that anger is carrying by showing some light of awareness, those emotions and feelings will start fading away.

It won't happen in one day but at least you can learn to recognize it, be a little more empathetic with yourself and provide yourself with a little extra dose of love to help you heal your emotions.

Love is the bandage which needs to be placed wherever you discover any unhealed part of yourself, whether it is anger, sadness or any other emotion that might come to the surface. But each time, be present (through breath work) and allow those emotions to pass away.

 If it's difficult to manage your emotions, take some time out: breathe deeply, walk in nature, get immersed in the beauty of nature here and now. But be present, don't suppress it, give them your love. Please don't run away from it, acknowledge it, and move on.

Fear separates you from infinite love. Fear makes you think that you are all alone and there is nobody there for you. It is a separation from love, from unity with divine being. It is a mind created phenomena. It doesn't understand things clearly; it eludes your judgment and thinking ability. It sometimes exaggerates things that don't even exist.

Fear has been present since decades on this planet. It amplifies everything and it comes from the feeling of always being under attack, need for safety or insecure about life situations.

The more we are in fear, the more we are separate from our soul's infinite potential and strength.

When fear starts increasing, it takes you away from love and makes you feel that you are unloved and on your own.

The universe (divine being) is always there with us, and universal love and its presence is the only thing that can make you feel safe, secure, and protected.

Let those fears which are crippling you, keeping you away from your infinite potential and strength go away. Allow yourself to release those fears as it doesn't serve you and is only keeping you limited and away from infinite love. Let those fears dissolve which originated in your childhood or in circumstances where you felt all alone.

We are never alone. We are always protected and guided by the universal forces (God). We are always surrounded with divine light of the universe which keeps us protected and makes us feel safe. That divine light is pure love energy, and it is the most powerful energy in the world. Don't think that fear has so much strength as love has.

Fear is a weak, low vibrational energy. Whereas love is the most powerful and has a higher vibrational energy. Hence fear cannot survive in the existence of love in our heart. So, keep expanding your love and hence fear will start decreasing until fear disappears completely.

Why does fear keep coming?
Fear is an old conditioning of mind and when it

feels that it's time to go, it starts affecting us more. It wants to conquer us and wants to keep us miserable as we have felt in fear. It knows that as you keep coming back to your true self, who you are, its existence becomes threatened.

Fear has kept feeding on your energy, depleting your energy and vibration. Would you want to stay in this zone of fear knowing that this fear is draining your energy and your life force (prana)? NO, you deserve a better life. You deserve a life full of joy, happiness, love, and peace.

Fear cripples you and drains your energy.
Love empowers you and expands your energy.

Now decide whether you want to stay in love or in fear? Let those fears go one by one as you keep filling your pitcher with love and remember you are always protected and guided. You are always safe as you belong to this world.

MANAGING EMOTIONS

Emotions are simple messengers telling you its need to be heard. Do not discard it, just give your love, give your care, and observe it and it will start disappearing. We are talking about our negative emotions and feelings. These emotions have been stored within our mind for decades and it might take time, but we must take charge of it.

Be patient with those emotions such as your fears, anger, anxiety, etc. as those emotions have been there with you for years and suppressing them will only make it worse. We all have been suppressing our emotions for so many years as we had no idea how to deal with it.

But suppressing those emotions only gets worse as it intensifies in a certain triggering situation every time. So now when these emotions arise; give it your love, awareness, presence and let it go.

Every problem present within us has been accumulated because of how little we have loved ourselves and how much we gave into other people's thoughts and judgments about us, depleting our self-esteem further. So, it's time to take charge of yourself.

AFFIRM:

- *I take charge of healing myself.*
- *I spread feelings of love in my mind and body.*
- *I am a loving being.*
- *I am divine.*
- *I am beautiful.*
- *I am magic. Magic resides within me.*
- *I am perfect.*
- *I got my power back.*
- *My powers are mine. I got it back.*

Do you feel motivated by reading this? Yes, you do. Because you are a powerful being, you just remind yourself daily till it resonates with you.

DAILY REMINDER:

- *I am a powerful being.*
- *My power resides within me.*
- *I respect my thoughts and emotions.*
- *I respect my body.*
- *I love myself completely and totally.*
- *I am a healed version of myself.*
- *I am proud of myself and my journey.*
- *I love myself.*
- *Thank you, universe (God), for always loving me and I love you- universe.*

Feel the love of the universe. *Divine light emerges*

inside your heart, filling you with unconditional love, compassion, and kindness. This is a pure and divine love and light energy, filling your heart with immense love spreading across your entire body. Feel this divine energy within you. You are glowing inside this pure light, filled with unconditional love that resides within you.

Love is here.

Feel it.

Gratitude unlocks the door to blessing and miracles in life. It showers infinite happiness and abundance upon you. Being grateful is the easiest way to enhance your vibrations and uplift your mood.it also helps us to be thankful for those infinite gifts we are blessed with, which we often neglect or forget and hence start criticizing and blaming our life and people around us.

Aren't you grateful for so many beautiful things around you? How do you feel when you look at nature, trees, beautiful chirping birds, soothing breeze passing through you? Look at the river flowing and supplying us with water.

Looking around trees always provides us with something or the other. Do you feel grateful towards them? Imagine if you don't have all these. Will you be alive? Then should we neglect our nature. Take time out to be grateful to the little, beautiful gifts of Mother Nature.

Look at the kind of house you are blessed with all the facilities available to you. See your loving family, so many people loving you, admiring you. Do you feel grateful towards them? Let's be grateful for those little things today.

Make gratitude an important aspect of your life and see how you feel daily. Always be grateful to the little things of life, even to yourself, your body: be grateful.

Isn't it amazing that these little things that we find in our day-to-day life can do wonders to us. The life that we are living is a dream for someone. Isn't it? We just need to acknowledge and start appreciating all the things and people around us with which we are blessed and let's realize their worth in order to live a life full of happiness and abundance.

HABITS

Anything that we do or steps that we take needs to be practiced. Let it form a habit for you, just like all the lazy habits that have been formed. Try doing anything suggested in this book for a minimum 21-30 days and see the results. Let these positive habits get inside every part of your body, allowing them to become an integral part of your life.

To heal, you need to allow yourself to change, to develop some new habits and practice these little things such as gratitude to form a habit of being grateful. Let go of your old patterns, your laziness, procrastination, if you are serious enough to heal yourself. Healing takes time, but when you heal, your soul evolves beautifully, becoming your true self, the one you are seeking

8

TAKE CHARGE OF YOUR THOUGHTS

Life is a roller coaster of all sorts of emotions, but a wise person is one who navigates the journey by just observing these events, situations, emotions, and thoughts. Always remember that you are not those thoughts and emotions.

Thoughts will come and go, let it pass through you instead of diving into the wave of thoughts, don't get drowned in it, just observe, and let it come and go. We assume that our thoughts are important, but in reality, this is an illusion, which separates us from our soul, our higher purpose.

Thoughts are just there to upgrade ourselves, get a higher vision, a higher purpose which can lead to prosperity. But when these thoughts create anger, sadness, irritation, anxiety, they are no longer productive. We must remember that when thoughts are not creating positive emotions, they are not productive thoughts.

Productive thoughts are one which helps you to get towards your highest purpose, making you feel happy, joyful, peaceful, which are your true nature. But what we are experiencing is not productive thoughts, it is just consuming your time, energy and making you feel miserable. Do you want to feel miserable? NO, then act.

Take action to save yourself from these unproductive thoughts, which are obstructing you to reach your highest goal, which is to be in a state of happiness and love. Take action to change those thoughts. The power lies with you, not with your thoughts.

You are more than your mind and thoughts, don't forget that. Your thoughts are not who you are and in order to know who you are, you need to silence your mind (i.e., your thoughts).

CONTROLLING THOUGHTS

> **MEDITATE** regularly on who you are. Ask yourself: "Who am I" while meditating. Let the answers come gradually.

> **DEEP BREATH WORK**: Be conscious of your breath as much as you can to increase your Prana Shakti (life force energy), it will help you in connecting with yourself and your body.

> **BE AWARE**, instead of being lost in your thoughts. Don't give your key of happiness to your thoughts. You can be happy without your thoughts. Think about it, we have just lost the way to be happy, although our happiness doesn't depend on our thoughts. When you observe simple things, you can be

happy without any reason. Do you remember any such instance? That's your true nature and that is how you are supposed to be every time, not once in a while.

When you feel happy without any reason, that is the true essence of who you truly are, that is your true state. Next time just don't think over it and enjoy that moment of happiness and it will expand gradually, and you will always be in that state of happiness, joy, peace, and ecstasy.

We are here to experience life, freedom, and unconditional love. By thinking so deeply at times, we lose the most beautiful things which are here for free: laughter, joy, happiness, love, kindness, freedom. Isn't it free?

And still, you want to become slave of your thoughts and drown in it. You need to decide. That's the first step. If the first step is not taken, how can we expect our entire life to be full of love and happiness? It can't be.

Look at babies. Aren't they happy in their little world with their little things? Do they need any occasion to smile and laugh? Do they need any occasion to be happy? No, because they are open to love, happiness, and joy in their life. And you put conditions to become happy, for instance, "if I get a promotion, I will be happy". Your happiness lies in some place in the future, which has not yet happened; instead of enjoying what you have now.

If you keep waiting for a future, which of course is not certain at all. Is there any guarantee that you will be happy once you get those things?

Your expectations and demands from life will change. Then when will you enjoy life? And later you will realize that you are near death bed and then all you can do is regret not enjoying life at all in those moments where you could have and there are so many such moments. You need to open your eyes to see those moments and not get drowned in your thoughts of misery and suffering.

9

AWARENESS IS THE KEY

BE PRESENT

Love yourself; treat yourself with dignity, respect, and love. Let any emotions come: be present, stay alert so that any thought doesn't come and keep increasing in your mind creating further suffering. It's similar to a garden which needs to be taken care of, if left unattended, weeds (negative thoughts) will start growing and spread all over the garden (mind) as no one was there to take care of the garden.

So, we need to be present. Especially with negative thoughts, we need to be alert, be present and see how one thought is arising and leading us towards anger, sadness, past traumas, repeating our victim stories. Hence, we need to be vigilant and alert, consciously deciding to be the king of our area which includes our mind (thoughts and feelings) and our body.

Tell those thoughts that you are in charge here and you cannot just roam around without permission. Tell them to function smoothly for a peaceful living and then slowly your thoughts will start listening, with the *power of your presence.*

Simply speaking, take deep breaths and be present and in this way, you will remain present inside your mind and body. Once you start being present which will take time and practice, you will start noticing the results. You will start noticing how your health is improving and you are healing all the pain in your body with your power of presence.

Awareness is necessary of what you are doing, where you are in the present moment. Be aware of your 'here and now'. Are you in the 'here and now'? Check yourself repeatedly and keep reminding yourself to be present. Keep doing dipsticks every now and then.

Am I in the 'here and now'? If yes, you are flowing with life and life flows along with you. If not, you are flowing against life and hence it flows against you creating more sufferings for you, being anxious and nervous, being angry, trying to control things, getting irritated, obsessive thinking, repetitive negative self-talk which becomes part of your life.

Do you want to live like that, or do you want to enjoy your present moment which has so much (positivity) to offer? You decide this. Decide what you want from life. You need to decide what kind of life you deserve.

So, are you flowing with life? Or are you flowing against life? It's your decision to make. It's our choice, everyday conscious choices which makes us who we want to be and what we take from life. Be in the flow of life, it has so much love to offer you, don't miss that by being lost in yourself and letting your mind take charge of you.

Take charge for yourself.
You deserve a life full of happiness and joy.
You deserve to be happy and full of love.

Let that unconditional love reach you. Allow the divine love to enter inside your heart every moment, be open to it always. That love is your right. We all deserve the divine love to flow into us every moment and when that love flows through you unstuck, you will see how happy and peaceful your life becomes. You will see how much love and joy you feel inside and thereby radiating that outside as well.

Open yourself to that divine unconditional love from the divine source of all creation. Surrender yourself to that pure love energy and let it flow through you, feeling you with positivity, happiness, love, joy, peacefulness, and calmness. Allow yourself to be open to infinite love from the supreme source of all creation. Flow with life.

Staying present is very necessary. It might not happen initially but practicing this principal matters. Even if for 10-15 minutes you are present in a day, you have sown the seeds and the results would soon be visible. Let your power of presence give you a new life. Try it.

10 STOP IDENTIFYING WITH YOUR EMOTIONS

We let our mind control us. We unintentionally allow it to feed on us and our energy. We have a desire to control how things happen in our life, but we are unable to control our own mind. Our mind requires control, not the external circumstances. We cannot control the outside world, but we can control the inside world.

If there is chaos inside, you will find it outside as well. But if there is peace within, you will find it outside because you will reflect that peace. You must start sowing seeds of positive thoughts and stop watering dead plants (unwanted emotions, thoughts, and feelings), by paying attention to it you are expanding it, you are creating further suffering for yourself.

Anger, fear, anxiety all these are mind created and it's not who you are, if you identify with it, these emotions will keep coming out sooner or later and create havoc in your life. Stop identifying yourself with these emotions. Stop saying that you are short-tempered, or you are always anxious, stressed, or depressed.

Not only are you identifying with it, but you are also manifesting it by repeating these statements so many times. Why can't you speak positively about yourself? Is it that difficult? Say out loud:

I am happiness.

I am joy.
I am at peace within me.
I am love.
I am lovable.
I am love and light.
I am joyous.
I am laughter.
I am powerful.
I am strong.
I am abundance.
I am prosperous.
I create my own life.
I am worthy of love and happiness.
I am worthy of success.
I am worthy of a beautiful life.

Plant the seeds of positivity and stop identifying yourself with what you are not. Remember if you don't decide and act, you will always find these things difficult.

But the seeds of positivity that you are sowing will grow and form into beautiful plants (Positive, prosperous, and abundant lifestyle) and that's how we start transforming by taking these little steps.

11

BE THE CHANGE

When your heart is filled with love, it lights up the entire room, filling it with love and more love. It is the key to connect with divine energy (God) as love has no language. It just spread on its own. It can lift anybody's mood. So be in love always, with yourself, with nature, your family, your life, your job and with all the creations of God.

Love dissolves all barriers. Where love is present, hate starts disappearing slowly and slowly. And one day you will realize you are all love. Everyone is capable of love; it's just that it disappears when life happens, with certain setbacks, betrayal, losing someone: you lose that spark of love you were born with.

But it is nobody's fault. Everyone is in the same situation. Even those who hate you somewhere hate themselves and that is reflected in their hatred towards you. So instead of dwelling in the same hate that you receive, flip the script, *switch your love mode on*, and love yourself a little more and move on by giving that person your blessings to heal soon.

It doesn't mean that you need to forget their hatred and hateful activities towards you, but it simply means to move away from it. So that you don't become the same person by spreading hate towards others.

BE THE CHANGE. When we hate others, there is some part within ourselves that we hate. Isn't it? Think about it!

How to be the change?

FORGIVE YOURSELF
FORGIVE OTHERS
MOVE ON
LET IT GO
INDULGE IN SELF-LOVE
SOAK IN NATURE

It's never simple to forgive someone because we don't want to let go. But you need to forgive if you want to be peaceful. Imagine holding a hot vessel and burning your own hand. You will be the one to suffer the most, when that hatred is alive within you.

Think about it! Aren't you suffering by keeping that hate alive? Don't suffer. You deserve better. You can consciously choose a better life by simply acknowledging your worth and what you deserve. Say out loud:
I am worthy.
I deserve love
I am worthy of love.
I deserve happiness.

These are simple statements, but very powerful, once you apply it in your life. Remember, you deserve a happy, loving, and peaceful life. So, stop being in victim mode and be your own hero.

Nobody is coming to rescue you. You have to rescue yourself. Are you ready to be your hero of life?

So, take your power back and affirm:
I take my power back. (repeat 3 times)
I love myself.
I deserve to be happy.
I deserve to live peacefully.

See your life changing with these simple, yet the most powerful steps that you can take for yourself in order to heal yourself. Healing is a deep work to transform oneself. It doesn't happen overnight. You will need practice; you will need constant love and support. You will need constant motivation and that too lies within yourself.

Recognize your wounds, accept it and start healing. Appreciate yourself for who you are and love yourself a little extra every day.

12

BE BEAUTIFUL FROM INSIDE

Today, be beautiful from inside. When you are beautiful inside, it reflects outside, shining in the entire world. Beautiful is not just an adjective to describe some object or people. It is a universal word, applicable to everyone, even to that person or object you call ugly.

Ugly is a wrong word that we have learned as we often describe or use this word to describe someone. But it's not right, it can hurt someone deeply. Beautiful is not a word, but also an emotion to describe how beautiful you are inside.

It's not the outer experience or appearance which describes beauty, it's the inner reflection of your nature. Your true nature of love, kindness, compassion, joy, tranquility. Your inner beauty lies in these expressions, in these natures of yours.

And everyone is beautiful inside; we just don't realize it. But if you peel those hard, outer layers, you will find how beautiful your soul is, pure soul and soul can never be ugly. It is those outer layers which have made us forget about our inner beauty, we need to find this inner beauty. Look at a newborn baby. Can you find anything ugly in that baby? No, because that baby is pure love, pure joy, pure happiness.

So how can you be ugly? You have just forgotten your inner beauty after becoming an adult, due to various reasons, which you know better. But are those reasons really important? Are those people or their judgment about you really important, which makes you look ugly? I don't think so.

So, dive into your inner beauty. Look inside without being critical for a second. Look at that inner beauty you were once as a baby and visualize how you feel, full of joy, energy, hope, happiness, and that innocence. This is your true nature.

Embrace that nature of yours, everything else that you believe about yourself is a lie. And don't worry you will shed those layers slowly and slowly. But for that you need to realize your inner beauty, your true nature, your soul qualities, which is your true essence and everything else, is a myth.

Everyday look into your eyes through a mirror and try to find that child full of love and hope. You will surely find it, which used to stay happy always, no matter what. Or look at a baby and play with him and try to find those qualities in you, those eyes filled with excitement, laughter, happiness, and love.

We are innately beautiful. We are not merely our body and emotions, we are soul; divine soul, pure soul coming from the Supreme Creator (God). Whenever you feel bad about yourself, always remember your beauty; that's who you are and that's who will remain even after death.

You are a pure soul.
You are a loving soul.
You are a peaceful soul.
You are a happy soul.

13

BEAUTY OF SOUL

Beauty is everywhere; nature's beauty, river's beauty, mountain's beauty and so is our soul's beauty. If you love mountains, snow, rivers then somewhere you are seeking the truth about your soul, the most beautiful creation of God.

Beauty of soul

Our soul is a beautiful garden. In a garden, we can see flying butterflies, flowers blooming, a breeze of fresh air, tiny green grasses and so many beautiful things around us. But maintaining the beauty of a garden is the responsibility of a gardener to make it look beautiful and not let any unwanted shrubs grow which can spoil its beauty. So is the case with our soul. It is our responsibility to take care of our garden and keep a check on it instead of letting the mind take control and allowing negative and unwanted thoughts and emotions to grow. Hence, we must be vigilant to take care of our soul and fill it with unconditional love.

Awareness of our thoughts and feelings is very important so that any adverse situation that arises, we nourish it with love and acceptance, so that it looks beautiful and help us to attract more positivity, abundance and prosperity in our life.

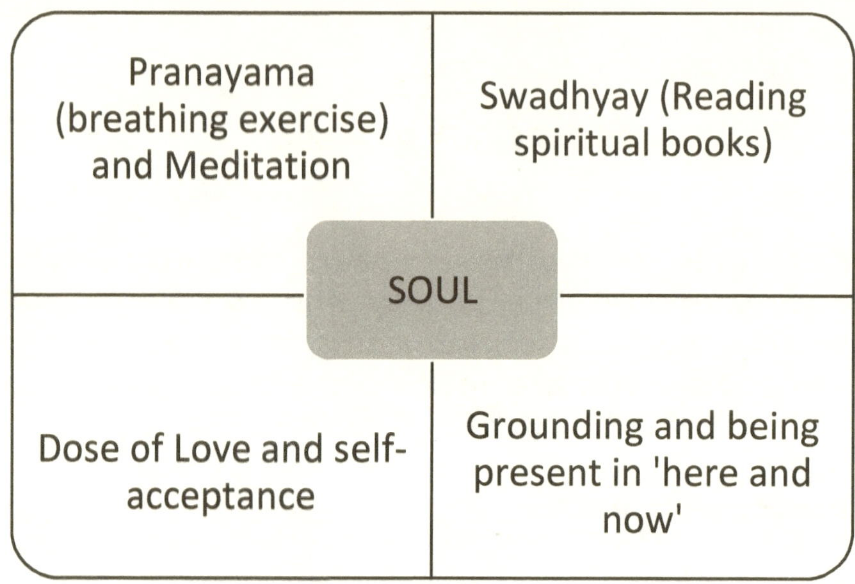

SOUL'S GARDEN

Make your garden beautiful. Once you take steps to nourish it, our soul knows what it needs; it will start giving you solutions in the form of people (healer), quotes, books or any other way which will resonate with you.

Listen to your soul's need; it will always guide you towards your highest good. Your soul knows everything which is good for you. Once you feel connected to your soul, you start feeling whole again. You will feel a sense of completeness, for which you were looking outside, you will find it within. All the answers lie within. Every solution is here, within, you just need to see and feel it. If not today, then tomorrow, but have faith, have trust in yourself and in the divine being(God) and surrender your worries to God and let him show the path of your highest good.

ABOUT THE AUTHOR

Yoga Trainer, psychologist & Author

Kavita Sharma is a passionate writer and yoga teacher dedicated to guiding others on their path to spirituality, healing, and self-discovery. Inspired by her own transformative journey, Kavita began writing as a powerful tool for personal healing and reflection. Through her heartfelt works, Kavita shares insights and practices to help readers connect deeply with their inner selves.

As a yoga teacher, Kavita loves nurturing both adults and children in their physical, mental, and spiritual growth through yoga. Her teachings often incorporate themes of mindfulness, inner peace, and holistic healing.

Outside of writing and teaching, Kavita hosts a podcast focused on spirituality and healing. With every episode, Kavita aims to create a space where listeners can explore profound ideas and find inspiration for their own journeys.

Follow yogicliving_kavita on Instagram to stay updated on her latest books, podcasts, and yoga classes!

When we have the courage to go inside, magic happens outside.

HEART TALK

When I started my healing journey, my only aim was to get what I lost, my unborn child due to miscarriage. I desperately wanted to get pregnant because that emptiness and void was somewhere eating me inside, I once again wanted to feel that connection with my baby, once again wanted to feel the maternal instinct that came in my life for a short time and it was the most beautiful feeling that I have ever experienced, feeling a life inside me, creating a life, feeling that unconditional love for a soul I haven't met was the most amazing feeling I experienced.

I was visiting doctors, looking for help here and there to see what was wrong with me in my last pregnancy which led to the loss and the more I was visiting doctors, the more I started hating my body and myself, without realizing that I myself was delaying my own pregnancy by creating self-hatred and by not trusting my body's ability to heal on its own. I didn't realize that that a woman is born with the most precious gift of a womb which itself represents creation and by creating those negative beliefs I was delaying the gift which I naturally possessed, to create.

Without knowing which path I should take, I started with my first "**Gayatri Puruscharan**";a nine days of *sadhna* of **Gayatri Mantra**,in which I was supposed to complete 24,000 japa in those 9 days with self-discipline. On the 9th day of my Puruscharan,my first breakthrough happened and **Reiki** (energy healing modality) came in my life, it helped me not only to heal myself but also to break own limited beliefs and the first step that I learned in my healing journey was to **love myself.** Without self-love, no healing can happen and to heal we must start loving and accepting ourself.Love is the strongest vibration present in the universe and when we start vibrating in the frequency of love, we start getting connected to the divine presence within us.

Loving oneself is not an easy process, it takes a lot of time, because we surrounded with layers of negative self-belief originated in our childhood which means it has become deep rooted and hence we need to change our beliefs by sowing new seeds within us: *seeds of positive thoughts.* If we can live so many years with our negative belief, then to bring transformation in our life, we can give some time to our healing, without giving up on ourself.You are the most beautiful version of yourself, so be proud of it.

Reading self-help books, positive books are a great way to begin with and my first book to healing was "you can heal your life" by Louis Hay, this book brought a lot of shift in my life and there began my journey of self-love. When we start healing ourselves, many aspect of our life starts unveiling before us, and one of that was healing my inner child. I discovered that there is a little child within me, waiting for me to reach out to her and the most important need of my inner child was to be loved and accepted by not other people, but by own self. I needed deep healing for my inner child and the way to reach her was to start showing her the love and acceptance that she always needed, but which she was unable to get because I always thought myself to be unworthy and became a people pleaser and in spite of my great efforts to be a good child and then to become a good adult, I realized others still had issues with me, were judgmental and criticized me when I needed their support. Isn't this strange after trying so hard to please others and behave obediently before others, people were still able to find fault within me and with this people pleasing behavior, I lost myself and left my inner child lonely and in a miserable condition. This realization made me break my negative self-beliefs one by one and brought me closer to my inner child: my happy space.

The more I healed, the more I explored aspects to heal and found that how I have created multiple health issues for myself by abusing my body with negative belief about myself and this was also the reason why I was not getting pregnant and once I started accepting my body and loving my body, I got pregnant as if no issues ever existed for me to conceive. But this was not the end, during my pregnancy I started having multiple health issues for which I had to be admitted into the hospital thrice. First time when I was admitted, it was a difficult time for me because the entire flash back of my last pregnancy came up before my eyes; fears and anxieties started flooding my mind. Soon this made me realized that I was lacking faith in myself and most importantly in the divine universal forces who were there along with me and hence finally I surrendered my worries to my Gurudev and the only thing that I was able to do was to remain positive and keep my faith intact. When we are strong with faith, magic automatically starts happening and hence my pregnancy continued although I had to take complete bed rest which was not something I wanted, but then I got more time to explore spirituality. Faith and surrender on my Gurudev helped me continue ahead because this time I deserved to be a mother. Whenever I started having doubts, I started journaling, speaking out positive affirmations and the most helpful thoughts was:

"I am the creator of my own destiny."(Pandit Shri Ram Sharma Acharya)

This affirmation kept me going. Affirmations are really very powerful because when we say something from our heart, and say it in the present tense, we are creating a different story, a better story for ourselves and the way we speak to ourselves and others have a profound effect on our subconscious mind.

As my pregnancy progressed, I thought now I am recovering and hence I can come out of my bed rest as staying in bed, in one room was slowly getting frustrated and just when I thought now my doctor is going to release me from my bed rest, another scan report came which revealed that my cervix size was very small, it was the same issue which I faced during my last pregnancy as well. I was strictly instructed not to move out of my bed when I was in my 6th month, my anxieties and fears cropped up like never before; the fear of once again repeating the same situation was really terrifying. I was uncertain about what was going to happen and I started questioning myself and my body, I was told that if I don't take proper rest, anytime I can deliver the baby which was very risky. I had no idea what to do any further as I felt that everything was getting out of my control. After a few days of staying in this panic mode, I decided that I won't give up and while I started journaling I realized how much I have blamed and criticized my body (specially my cervix) for the last incident and that needed to be healed.

Hence I decided to give positive affirmations to my body:

I love you my body. I accept you my body exactly as you are.

I love you my cervix. I accept you as you are.

I started doing this practice every day in the morning and also included gratitude in my life. I started giving gratitude to my body, to my baby in womb, for my health and for my safe and normal delivery.

"Thank you my cervix for carrying my baby with love

and care. I love you."

Sometimes we do fail to acknowledge that the moment we start thinking negative and form negative belief system, we form so many illnesses within us, we abuse our body, and we take it for granted. Isn't it?

Finally, those affirmations and gratitude helped me reach my 9th month which seemed impossible for my doctor because they expected that I could deliver any month. I not only delivered my baby girl full term but also had normal delivery which was a miracle as I was not allowed to walk and prepare myself for a normal delivery. This was the miracle of loving my body. It was possible because of faith and surrender to the divine forces.Infact,I didn't have to bear labor pain for a long time, my spirit guides and angels were there with me, supporting me and loving me.Till today, I thank this day because of so many miracles and the most miraculous moment was to hold my baby girl in my arms as I was blessed with the most precious gift of the world, my very own little angel.

After the delivery, I was busy with my new born baby. Just like every mother, I had no time for anything but slowly I felt something missing in my life and soon after 6-7 months of my delivery, I once again Gayatri Mantra chanting which once gain brought some light in my life because life is not just about material things, it is beyond that, as we are born for a greater purpose, so I once again started taking out time for myself indulged in my healing and that is when Angel Therapy came in my life and then I realized how angels and their support have always been there with me during my most difficult time, during my pregnancy and when I went to my Gurudev's Ashram, I discovered all the signs of angels that I was receiving in those last 2 years. He was always there with me in his astral form. I am deeply grateful to my Gurudev for his presence in my life and for bringing light in my life in the form of spirituality which made me connect with my inner self.

Initially I felt that healing will make me all positive person and I will always be happy and peaceful. But as I started to work on myself, many negative thoughts and feelings started coming in, such as anger, anxiety, fear, sadness, when I started experiencing all these feelings again, I felt that healing is not working out for me and I should stop doing it because I was feeling just the opposite. I was somewhat fighting with these emotions, which made it worse because the more I was fighting, the more I was experiencing these emotions. Even after feeling like to give up on myself for so many times I didn't give up. Soon I realized that I shouldn't fight these emotions, I am the one who have created though unintentionally, hence I started doing Swadhyay (reading spiritual books), indulged myself into more positive actions. There were two things that I realized. Firstly, I should learn to embrace my positive and negative side and this is only possible when I will show love and acceptance by shedding light on those hidden aspects of myself which I was not accepting. Secondly, when everything seems dark and we feel like to give up, take refuge of positive books, their light can help us to move ahead.

I am still trying to learn something new each day, by doing my spiritual practices consistently specially Gayatri Mantra chanting. We are all going to experience challenges in our spiritual journey, never give up on yourself and keep your faith intact on God in which you believe. I realized that there is only one religion in this world which is "humanity" and to access it we must tap into "spirituality", which is to recognize divinity stored within us. When you are able to connect with yourself, your divinity will rise.

All the best on your spiritual journey of finding yourself.

An introduction to my Gurudev

Pandit Acharya Shriram Sharma (1911-1990) was said to be the simplest of men. Throughout his life he owned only two sets of clothes. He began every day with a pad of paper and a ball point pen. And his spiritual practice, throughout his life, was the recitation of a single mantra: **Gayatri Mantra**.

And yet, wherever he went, he sowed seeds that would grow into a mighty movement. Upon the basis of his simplicity was established the integrity of a movement that would renounce the addictions of modern life. With his pen and paper, he wrote discourses on every aspect of human culture and wellbeing that would be translated into 13 languages. And by means of his mantra recitation, he laid the energetic foundation for a new human culture based on the practices and wisdom of ancestral India.

In his own time, he was revered as a visionary, a prophet and a world reforming saint.

(Taken from: **The Real joy of Entertainment by PANDIT SHRIRAM SHARMA ACHARYA**)

Gayatri is wisdom

Goddess Gayatri is the supreme creative energy of the divine. It endows its devotee with true wisdom. A subtle, uninterrupted current of divine energy starts flowing through the inner being of the devotee, cleansing his intellect, mind and emotions of the perverse, perverted and dark thoughts feelings and desires.

The *Sadhna* of *Gayatri* is worship of supreme knowledge. The effect of sincere and steadfast *Gayatri Sadhna* is swift and miraculous in purifying, harmonizing and steadying the mind and thus establishing unshakable inner peace and a sense of joy-filled calm even in the face of grave trials and tribulations in the outer life of *Sadhak*.

Gayatri Mantra manifested itself through *Brahma* in the beginning of the creation.*Brahma* interpreted it by four mouths in the form of four *Vedas*. This knowledge is for the benefit of all mankind.Pesons of all castes, creeds and of both sexes have equal right to adopt *Gayatri Mantra* as means of their *Sadhana.*

Righteous *wisdom* starts emerging as soon as *Jap* of this *Mantra* is taken up as a *Sadhna.*

Om Bhurbhuvah Svah Tat Savitur Varenyam Bhargo Devasya Dhimahi Dhiyo Yo Nah Prachodayat.

It is a prayer to the Almighty Supreme God, the Creator of entire cosmos, and the essence of our life existence, who removes all our pains and sufferings and grants happiness beseeching. His divine grace to imbibe within us His divinity and brilliance, which may purify us and guide our righteous wisdom on the right path.

Those who tread this path pass joyously through life and ultimately reach the ultimate goal of God realization.

Foundation of New Era through Gayatri Mantra

Gayatri is also known as *Adya Shakti* because *Brahma,*who was born from the Navel lotus of *Vishnu,*was directed to take support of this *Maha Mantra* for creation.*Brahma* worshipped it and performed *Tap* and brought forth all animate and inanimate creation.

This great power will now be known as the power of a *new golden era* because the deadly poisons permeating the atmosphere,environment and minds and hearts of human beings can be neutralized only with the help of collective *Sadhna* of this *Mantra.*The new era is also descending in the form of *Pragya* (enlightened intelligence) movement or *Pragyavtar.*The next era will be known as **Pragyayug** (era of enlightenment).It can also be called *Satyug.*

(Taken from: **Super Science of Gayatri by PANDIT SHRIRAM SHARMA ACHARYA)**

Atmadev is not just a character—it is the divine spark within each of us.
This book invites readers on a profound inward journey to discover their
true nature, guided by the essence of Atmadev, the Higher Self. Through
reflective prose and spiritual insight, it explores timeless questions:
- Who am I?
- What is my true nature?
- Am I merely a body and mind—or something deeper?
Rather than seeking answers in the external world, the book encourages
readers to turn inward, connect with their divine intuition, and awaken
to the truth that already resides within. Atmadev becomes both guide
and mirror, illuminating the path of self-realization, detachment, and
spiritual awakening.
Whether you call it the soul, the Divine Self, or pure consciousness,
Atmadev is the voice of inner wisdom that leads you home.

Dive into the inner journey of Self-reflection and transformation.